100 POEMS EVERY CHILD
-and adult-
SHOULD KNOW

100 POEMS EVERY CHILD
-and adult-
SHOULD KNOW

A collection of poems by some of the most famous authors, that will make both children and adults fall in love with the magic of Classic Poetry.

Valeska Matti

ISBN-13: 978-90-832446-0-0
ISBN-10: 90-832446-0-1

*Dedicated to all authors who gifted us
the magic of their poetry.*

TABLE OF CONTENTS

PREFACE

The universe of Classic Poetry is so vast and rich, that any attempt to put a collection together -a subjective exercise by definition- will likely fail to satisfy more than a few poetry lovers. Nevertheless, I got inspired to proceed with this quest after reading Mary E. Burt's anthology "Poems every Child Should Know", published in 1904. Many of the pieces you will find here come from her impeccable selection, which she aimed at school-age children. Remember that those were days when it was the norm to read and memorize verses at school, and discussions about *what did they mean with that?* were a weekly exercise in class.

I, however, have removed many of the longer and more complex poems from her anthology and added several other pieces from some of my favorite writers of English poetry of the past centuries. You will also find a few famous anonymous works, such as the old New Zealand folk song "Soon May the Wellerman Come", nowadays very popular on social media platforms. I have distributed the poems in seven sections, following a rather loose definition of seven "themes". You will probably find poems that could belong to more than one section, that's how multifaceted poetry can be.

Amongst several others, the following famous authors are represented in this collection:

Alexander Pope - Charles Dickens - Elizabeth Barrett Browning - Robert Burns - Rudyard Kipling - Felicia Hemans - Lewis Carrol - Alfred Tennyson - Emily Elizabeth Dickinson - Anne Bradstreet - Robert Browning - Eugene Field - Walt Whitman - Sara Teasdale

As you move on from section to section, you will realize that the complexity of the pieces will tend to increase, as will the length of some of them. When reading this book with or to the littlest ones, please be mindful of the last two sections, particularly the final one, as some of the pieces can be somewhat somber in tone. The notion of departing from this life is present in a few of them, in some cases more explicitly than in others. I had a long internal

debate about how deep to go with the selection of poems with a "negative" plot. I excluded quite a few wonderful pieces because they were too descriptive in matters of faith or tragedy. Nonetheless, I concluded that even the youngest ones out there are nowadays exposed to both real and fictional "negative" content daily, with ever-present wars, conflicts, accidents, and tragedy in the news, song videos, TV shows, and even in games. So, I am letting this be a good reason to remind everyone that it is also possible to write beautifully about sadness.

In this digital era we are living in, we have little to no exposure to poetry, and our single source of metaphors and rhymes is found in -frequently superficial- song lyrics. Outside of music, the magic we can achieve with words is neither valued nor present anymore. Many contemporary poets are creating exquisite pieces, but the exposure they get is limited.

This is my humble tribute to poetry. It is an attempt to bring Classic Poetry back to your tables. Whether you choose to read the poems in strict order, randomly selecting a page or searching for a theme or title which resonates with your state of mind at a particular moment, whether you read one poem a week or the complete collection in one sitting, I please ask you to help me spread the word, that poetry can still be magical, and that many classical pieces, archaic English and all, can be as relevant today as they were 300 years ago.

I sincerely hope you will enjoy this selection.

Valeska Matti

I

OF LIFE AND LOVE

1. HIDDEN LOVE

I hid the love within my heart,
And lit the laughter in my eyes,
That when we meet he may not know
My love that never dies.

But sometimes when he dreams at night
Of fragrant forests green and dim,
It may be that my love crept out
And brought the dream to him.

And sometimes when his heart is sick
And suddenly grows well again,
It may be that my love was there
To free his life of pain.

SARA TEASDALE

2. A BOUQUET

A blossom pink, a blossom blue,
Make all there is in love so true.
'Tis fit, methinks, my heart to move,
To give it thee, sweet girl, I love!
Now, take it, dear, this morn and wear
A wreath of beauty in thy hair;
Think on it, when from bliss we part -
The emblem of my wooing heart!

EDWARD SMYTH JONES

3. A MAIDEN

Oh if I were the velvet rose
Upon the red rose vine,
I'd climb to touch his window
And make his casement fine.

And if I were the little bird
That twitters on the tree,
All day I'd sing my love for him
Till he should harken me.

But since I am a maiden
I go with downcast eyes,
And he will never hear the songs
That he has turned to sighs.

And since I am a maiden
My love will never know
That I could kiss him with a mouth
More red than roses blow.

SARA TEASDALE

4. CUPID DROWNED

T'other day as I was twining
Roses, for a crown to dine in,
What, of all things, 'mid the heap,
Should I light on, fast asleep,
But the little desperate elf,
The tiny traitor, Love, himself!
By the wings I picked him up
Like a bee, and in a cup
Of my wine I plunged and sank him,
Then what d'ye think I did?--I drank him.
Faith, I thought him dead. Not he!
There he lives with tenfold glee;
And now this moment with his wings
I feel him tickling my heart-strings.

LEIGH HUNT

5. CUPID STUNG

Cupid once upon a bed
Of roses laid his weary head;
Luckless urchin, not to see
Within the leaves a slumbering bee.
The bee awak'd--with anger wild
The bee awak'd, and stung the child.
Loud and piteous are his cries;
To Venus quick he runs, he flies;
"Oh, Mother! I am wounded through--
I die with pain--in sooth I do!
Stung by some little angry thing,
Some serpent on a tiny wing--
A bee it was--for once, I know,
I heard a rustic call it so."
Thus he spoke, and she the while
Heard him with a soothing smile;
Then said, "My infant, if so much
Thou feel the little wild bee's touch,
How must the heart, ah, Cupid! be,
The hapless heart that's stung by thee!"

THOMAS MOORE

6. CUPID AND MY CAMPASBE

Cupid and my Campasbe played
At cards for kisses. Cupid paid.
He stakes his quiver, bow and arrows,
His mother's doves and team of sparrows.
Loses them, too; then down he throws
The coral of his lips, the rose
Growing on his cheek, but none knows how;
With them the crystal of his brow,
And then the dimple of his chin.
All these did my Campasbe win.
At last he set her both his eyes;
She won and Cupid blind did rise.
Oh, Love, hath she done this to thee!
What shall, alas, become of me!

JOHN LYLY

7. A DRINKING SONG

Wine comes in at the mouth
And love comes in at the eye;
That's all we shall know for truth
Before we grow old and die.
I lift the glass to my mouth,
I look at you, and I sigh.

WILLIAM BUTLER YEATS

8. THE TOURNAMENT

Bright shone the lists, blue bent the skies,
And the knights still hurried amain
To the tournament under the ladies' eyes,
Where the jousters were Heart and Brain.

Flourished the trumpets, entered Heart,
A youth in crimson and gold;
Flourished again; Brain stood apart,
Steel-armoured, dark and cold.

Heart's palfrey caracoled gaily round,
Heart tra-li-ra'd merrily;
But Brain sat still, with never a sound,
So cynical-calm was he.

Heart's helmet-crest bore favours three
From his lady's white hand caught;
While Brain wore a plumeless casque; not he
Or favour gave or sought.

The trumpet blew; Heart shot a glance
To catch his lady's eye.
But Brain gazed straight ahead, his lance
To aim more faithfully.

They charged, they struck; both fell, both bled;
Brain rose again, ungloved;
Heart, dying, smiled and faintly said,
"My love to my beloved."

SIDNEY LANIER

9. A BOY'S SONG

Where the pools are bright and deep,
Where the gray trout lies asleep,
Up the river and o'er the lea,
That's the way for Billy and me.

Where the blackbird sings the latest,
Where the hawthorn blooms the sweetest,
Where the nestlings chirp and flee,
That's the way for Billy and me.

Where the mowers mow the cleanest,
Where the hay lies thick and greenest,
There to trace the homeward bee,
That's the way for Billy and me.

Where the hazel bank is steepest,
Where the shadow falls the deepest,
Where the clustering nuts fall free.
That's the way for Billy and me.

Why the boys should drive away,
Little sweet maidens from the play,
Or love to banter and fight so well,
That's the thing I never could tell.

But this I know, I love to play,
Through the meadow, among the hay;
Up the water and o'er the lea,
That's the way for Billy and me.

JAMES HOGG

10. THE BABIE

Nae shoon to hide her tiny taes,
Nae stockin' on her feet;
Her supple ankles white as snaw,
Or early blossoms sweet.

Her simple dress o' sprinkled pink,
Her double, dimplit chin,
Her puckered lips, and baumy mou',
With na ane tooth within.

Her een sae like her mither's een,
Twa gentle, liquid things;
Her face is like an angel's face:
We're glad she has nae wings.

JEREMIAH EAMES RANKIN

11. A NEW ARRIVAL

There came to port last Sunday night
The queerest little craft,
Without an inch of rigging on;
I looked and looked and laughed.
It seemed so curious that she
Should cross the Unknown water,
And moor herself right in my room,
My daughter, O my daughter!

Yet by these presents witness all
She's welcome fifty times,
And comes consigned to Hope and Love
And common-meter rhymes.
She has no manifest but this,
No flag floats o'er the water,
She's too new for the British Lloyds--
My daughter, O my daughter!

Ring out, wild bells, and tame ones too!
Ring out the lover's moon!
Ring in the little worsted socks!
Ring in the bib and spoon!
Ring out the muse! ring in the nurse!
Ring in the milk and water!
Away with paper, pen, and ink--
My daughter, O my daughter!

GEORGE W. CABLE

12. A WISH

Mine be a cot beside the hill;
A bee-hive's hum shall soothe my ear;
A willowy brook that turns a mill
With many a fall shall linger near.

The swallow, oft, beneath my thatch
Shall twitter from her clay-built nest;
Oft shall the pilgrim lift the latch,
And share my meal, a welcome guest.

Around my ivied porch shall spring
Each fragrant flower that drinks the dew;
And Lucy, at her wheel, shall sing
In russet gown and apron blue.

The village church among the trees,
Where first our marriage-vows were given,
With merry peals shall swell the breeze
And point with taper spire to Heaven.

SAMUEL ROGERS

13. I REMEMBER, I REMEMBER

I remember, I remember
The house where I was born,
The little window where the sun
Came peeping in at morn;
He never came a wink too soon
Nor brought too long a day;
But now, I often wish the night
Had borne my breath away.

I remember, I remember
The roses, red and white,
The violets, and the lily-cups--
Those flowers made of light!
The lilacs where the robin built,
And where my brother set
The laburnum on his birthday,--
The tree is living yet!

I remember, I remember
Where I was used to swing,
And thought the air must rush as fresh
To swallows on the wing;
My spirit flew in feathers then
That is so heavy now,
And summer pools could hardly cool
The fever on my brow.

I remember, I remember
The fir trees dark and high;
I used to think their slender tops
Were close against the sky:
It was a childish ignorance,
But now 'tis little joy
To know I'm farther off from Heaven
Than when I was a boy.

THOMAS HOOD

14. A HAPPY LIFE

How happy is he born and taught
That serveth not another's will;
Whose armour is his honest thought,
And simple truth his utmost skill!

Whose passions not his master's are,
Whose soul is still prepared for death,
Not tied unto the world with care
Of public fame, or private breath.

SIR HENRY WOTTON

II

OF EARTH AND SKY

15. THE BROOK

I chatter, chatter, as I flow
To join the brimming river;
For men may come and men may go,
But I go on forever.

I wind about, and in and out,
With here a blossom sailing,
And here and there a lusty trout,
And here and there a grayling.

I steal by lawns and grassy plots,
I slide by hazel covers;
I move the sweet forget-me-nots
That grow for happy lovers.

I slip, I slide, I gloom, I glance,
Among my skimming swallows;
I make the netted sunbeams dance
Against my sandy shallows.

I murmur under moon and stars
In brambly wildernesses;
I linger by my shingly bars;
I loiter round my cresses.

And out again I curve and flow
To join the brimming river;
For men may come and men may go,
But I go on forever.

ALFRED TENNYSON

16. THE STAR

A white star born in the evening glow
Looked to the round green world below,
And saw a pool in a wooded place
That held like a jewel her mirrored face.
She said to the pool: "Oh, wondrous deep,
I love you, I give you my light to keep.
Oh, more profound than the moving sea
That never has shown myself to me!
Oh, fathomless as the sky is far,
Hold forever your tremulous star!"
But out of the woods as night grew cool
A brown pig came to the little pool;
It grunted and splashed and waded in
And the deepest place but reached its chin.
The water gurgled with tender glee
And the mud churned up in it turbidly.
The star grew pale and hid her face
In a bit of floating cloud like lace.

SARA TEASDALE

17. TWINKLE, TWINKLE, LITTLE STAR

Twinkle, twinkle, little star!
How I wonder what you are,
Up above the world so high,
Like a diamond in the sky.

When the glorious sun is set,
When the grass with dew is wet,
Then you show your little light,
Twinkle, twinkle all the night.

In the dark-blue sky you keep,
And often through my curtains peep,
For you never shut your eye,
Till the sun is in the sky.

As your bright and tiny spark
Guides the traveller in the dark,
Though I know not what you are,
Twinkle, twinkle, little star!

JANE TAYLOR

18. THE RAINBOW

Triumphal arch, that fills the sky
When storms prepare to part,
I ask not proud Philosophy
To teach me what thou art.

Still seem, as to my childhood's sight,
A midway station given,
For happy spirits to alight,
Betwixt the earth and heaven.

THOMAS CAMPBELL

19. THE FROST

The Frost looked forth, one still, clear night,
And whispered, "Now I shall be out of sight;
So through the valley and over the height,
In silence I'll take my way:
I will not go on with that blustering train,
The wind and the snow, the hail and the rain,
Who make so much bustle and noise in vain,
But I'll be as busy as they."

Then he flew to the mountain and powdered its crest;
He lit on the trees, and their boughs he dressed
In diamond beads--and over the breast
Of the quivering lake he spread
A coat of mail, that it need not fear
The downward point of many a spear
That hung on its margin far and near,
Where a rock could rear its head.

He went to the windows of those who slept,
And over each pane, like a fairy, crept;
Wherever he breathed, wherever he slept,
By the light of the moon were seen
Most beautiful things--there were flowers and trees;
There were bevies of birds and swarms of bees;
There were cities with temples and towers, and these
All pictured in silver sheen!

But he did one thing that was hardly fair;
He peeped in the cupboard, and finding there
That all had forgotten for him to prepare--
"Now just to set them a-thinking,
I'll bite this basket of fruit," said he,
"This costly pitcher I'll burst in three,
And the glass of water they've left for me
Shall '_tchich!_' to tell them I'm drinking."

HANNAH FLAGG GOULD

20. THE WIND AND THE MOON

Said the Wind to the Moon, "I will blow you out,
        You stare -- In the air
        Like a ghost in a chair,
Always looking what I am about--
I hate to be watched; I'll blow you out."

The Wind blew hard, and out went the Moon.
        So, deep -- On a heap
        Of clouds to sleep,
Down lay the Wind, and slumbered soon,
Muttering low, "I've done for that Moon."

He turned in his bed; she was there again!
        On high -- In the sky,
        With her one ghost eye,
The Moon shone white and alive and plain.
Said the Wind, "I will blow you out again."

The Wind blew hard, and the Moon grew dim.
        "With my sledge, and my wedge,
        I have knocked off her edge!
If only I blow right fierce and grim,
The creature will soon be dimmer than dim."

He blew and he blew, and she thinned to a thread.
        "One puff -- More's enough
        To blow her to snuff!
One good puff more where the last was bred,
And glimmer, glimmer, glum will go the thread."

He blew a great blast, and the thread was gone
In the air -- Nowhere
Was a moonbeam bare;
Far off and harmless the shy stars shone--
Sure and certain the Moon was gone!

The Wind he took to his revels once more;
On down, In town,
Like a merry-mad clown,
He leaped and hallooed with whistle and roar--
"What's that?" The glimmering thread once more!

He flew in a rage--he danced and blew;
But in vain -- Was the pain
Of his bursting brain;
For still the broader the Moon-scrap grew,
The broader he swelled his big cheeks and blew.

Slowly she grew--till she filled the night,
And shone -- On her throne
In the sky alone,
A matchless, wonderful silvery light,
Radiant and lovely, the queen of the night.

Said the Wind: "What a marvel of power am I
With my breath, Good faith!
I blew her to death--
First blew her away right out of the sky--
Then blew her in; what strength have I!"

But the Moon she knew nothing about the affair;
For high -- In the sky,
With her one white eye,
Motionless, miles above the air,
She had never heard the great Wind blare.

GEORGE MACDONALD

21. BECLOUDED

The sky is low, the clouds are mean,
A travelling flake of snow
Across a barn or through a rut
Debates if it will go.

A narrow wind complains all day
How some one treated him;
Nature, like us, is sometimes caught
Without her diadem.

EMILY ELIZABETH DICKINSON

22. THE FOUR ELEMENTS
(A FRAGMENT)

The Fire, Air, Earth and Water did contest
Which was the strongest, noblest and the best,
Who was of greatest use and might'est force;
In placide Terms they thought now to discourse,
That in due order each her turn should speak;
But enmity this amity did break
All would be chief, and all scorn'd to be under
Whence issu'd winds & rains, lightning & thunder.
The quaking earth did groan, the Sky lookt black
The Fire, the forced Air, in sunder crack;
The sea did threat the heav'ns, the heavn's the earth,
All looked like a Chaos or new birth:
Fire broyled Earth, & scorched Earth it choaked
Both by their darings, water so provoked
That roaring in it came, and with its source
Soon made the Combatants abate their force
The rumbling hissing: puffing was so great
The worlds confusion, it did seem to threat
Till gentle Air, Contention so abated
That betwixt hot and cold, she arbritrated
The others difference, being less did cease
All storms now laid, and they in perfect peace
That Fire should first begin, the rest consent,
The noblest and most active Element

(...)

ANNE BRADSTREET

23. JUNE

What is so rare as a day in June?
Then, if ever, come perfect days;
Then Heaven tries the earth if it be in tune,
And over it softly her warm ear lays:
Whether we look, or whether we listen,
We hear life murmur, or see it glisten;

Every clod feels a stir of might,
An instinct within it that reaches and towers,
And, groping blindly above it for light,
Climbs to a soul in grass and flowers;
The flush of life may well be seen
Thrilling back over hills and valleys;
The cowslip startles in meadows green.
The buttercup catches the sun in its chalice,
And there's never a leaf nor a blade too mean
To be some happy creature's palace;

The little bird sits at his door in the sun,
Atilt like a blossom among the leaves,
And lets his illumined being o'errun
With the deluge of summer it receives;

His mate feels the eggs beneath her wings,
And the heart in her dumb breast flutters and sings;
He sings to the wide world, and she to her nest,--
In the nice ear of Nature which song is the best?

JAMES RUSSELL LOWELL

24. PIPPA

The year's at the spring,
The day's at the morn;
Morning's at seven;
The hillside's dew pearled;

The lark's on the wing;
The snail's on the thorn;
God's in His heaven--
All's right with the world!

ROBERT BROWNING

III

OF FLORA AND FAUNA

25. THE VIOLET

Down in a green and shady bed
A modest violet grew;
Its stalk was bent, it hung its head,
As if to hide from view.

And yet it was a lovely flower,
No colours bright and fair;
It might have graced a rosy bower,
Instead of hiding there.

Yet there it was content to bloom,
In modest tints arrayed;
And there diffused its sweet perfume,
Within the silent shade.

Then let me to the valley go,
This pretty flower to see;
That I may also learn to grow
In sweet humility.

JANE TAYLOR

26. THE LAST ROSE OF SUMMER

'Tis the last rose of summer
Left blooming alone;
All her lovely companions
Are faded and gone;
No flower of her kindred,
No rose-bud is nigh,
To reflect back her blushes,
Or give sigh for sigh.

I'll not leave thee, thou lone one!
To pine on the stem;
Since the lovely are sleeping,
Go, sleep thou with them.
Thus kindly I scatter
Thy leaves o'er the bed
Where thy mates of the garden
Lie scentless and dead.

So soon may I follow,
When friendships decay,
And from Love's shining circle
The gems drop away.
When true hearts lie withered,
And fond ones are flown,
O! who would inhabit
This bleak world alone?

THOMAS MOORE

27. LITTLE WHITE LILY

Little White Lily
Sat by a stone,
Drooping and waiting
Till the sun shone.
Little White Lily
Sunshine has fed;
Little White Lily
Is lifting her head.

Little White Lily
Said: "It is good
Little White Lily's
Clothing and food."
Little White Lily
Dressed like a bride!
Shining with whiteness,
And crownèd beside!

Little White Lily
Drooping with pain,
Waiting and waiting
For the wet rain.
Little White Lily
Holdeth her cup;
Rain is fast falling
And filling it up.

Little White Lily
Said: "Good again,
When I am thirsty
To have the nice rain.
Now I am stronger,
Now I am cool;
Heat cannot burn me,
My veins are so full."

Little White Lily
Smells very sweet;
On her head sunshine,
Rain at her feet.
Thanks to the sunshine,
Thanks to the rain,
Little White Lily
Is happy again.

GEORGE MACDONALD

28. BUTTERCUPS AND DAISIES

Buttercups and daisies,
Oh, the pretty flowers,
Coming ere the spring time,
To tell of sunny hours.
While the tree are leafless,
While the fields are bare,
Buttercups and daisies
Spring up here and there.

Ere the snowdrop peepeth,
Ere the crocus bold,
Ere the early primrose
Opes its paly gold,
Somewhere on the sunny bank
Buttercups are bright;
Somewhere 'mong the frozen grass
Peeps the daisy white.

Little hardy flowers,
Like to children poor,
Playing in their sturdy health
By their mother's door,
Purple with the north wind,
Yet alert and bold;
Fearing not, and caring not,
Though they be a-cold!

What to them is winter!
What are stormy showers!
Buttercups and daisies
Are these human flowers!
He who gave them hardships
And a life of care,
Gave them likewise hardy strength
And patient hearts to bear.

MARY HOWITT

29. WOODMAN, SPARE THAT TREE!

Woodman, spare that tree!
Touch not a single bough!
In youth it sheltered me,
And I'll protect it now.
'Twas my forefather's hand
That placed it near his cot;
There, woodman, let it stand,
Thy ax shall harm it not.

That old familiar tree,
Whose glory and renown
Are spread o'er land and sea--
And wouldst thou hew it down?
Woodman, forbear thy stroke!
Cut not its earth-bound ties;
Oh, spare that agèd oak
Now towering to the skies!

When but an idle boy,
I sought its grateful shade;
In all their gushing joy
Here, too, my sisters played.
My mother kissed me here;
My father pressed my hand--
Forgive this foolish tear,
But let that old oak stand.

My heart-strings round thee cling,
Close as thy bark, old friend!
Here shall the wild-bird sing,
And still thy branches bend.
Old tree! the storm still brave!
And, woodman, leave the spot;
While I've a hand to save,
Thy ax shall harm it not.

GEORGE POPE MORRIS

30. THE IVY GREEN

O, a dainty plant is the ivy green,
That creepeth o'er ruins old!
Of right choice food are his meals, I ween,
In his cell so lone and cold.
The walls must be crumbled, the stones decayed.
To pleasure his dainty whim;
And the mouldering dust that years have made
Is a merry meal for him.
  Creeping where no life is seen,
  A rare old plant is the ivy green.

Fast he stealeth on, though he wears no wings,
And a staunch old heart has he!
How closely he twineth, how tight he clings
To his friend, the huge oak tree!
And slyly he traileth along the ground,
And his leaves he gently waves,
And he joyously twines and hugs around
The rich mould of dead men's graves.
  Creeping where no life is seen,
  A rare old plant is the ivy green.

Whole ages have fled, and their works decayed,
And nations have scattered been;
But the stout old ivy shall never fade
From its hale and hearty green.
The brave old plant in its lonely days
Shall fatten upon the past;
For the stateliest building man can raise
Is the ivy's food at last.
  Creeping where no life is seen,
  A rare old plant is the ivy green.

CHARLES DICKENS

31. MOLY

Traveller, pluck a stem of moly,
If thou touch at Circe's isle,--
Hermes' moly, growing solely
To undo enchanter's wile!
When she proffers thee her chalice,--
Wine and spices mixed with malice,--
When she smites thee with her staff
To transform thee, do thou laugh!
Safe thou art if thou but bear
The least leaf of moly rare.
Close it grows beside her portal,
Springing from a stock immortal,
Yes! and often has the Witch
Sought to tear it from its niche;
But to thwart her cruel will
The wise God renews it still.
Though it grows in soil perverse,
Heaven hath been its jealous nurse,
And a flower of snowy mark
Springs from root and sheathing dark;
Kingly safeguard, only herb
That can brutish passion curb!
Some do think its name should be
Shield-Heart, White Integrity.
Traveller, pluck a stem of moly,
If thou touch at Circe's isle,--
Hermes' moly, growing solely
To undo enchanter's wile!

EDITH M. THOMAS

32. THE SKYLARK

Bird of the wilderness,
Blithesome and cumberless,
Sweet be thy matin o'er moorland and lea!
Emblem of happiness,
Blest is thy dwelling-place--
Oh, to abide in the desert with thee!

Wild is thy lay and loud,
Far in the downy cloud,
Love gives it energy, love gave it birth.
Where, on thy dewy wing,
Where art thou journeying?
Thy lay is in heaven, thy love is on earth.

O'er fell and fountain sheen,
O'er moor and mountain green,
O'er the red streamer that heralds the day,
Over the cloudlet dim,
Over the rainbow's rim,
Musical cherub, soar, singing, away!

Then, when the gloaming comes,
Low in the heather blooms
Sweet will thy welcome and bed of love be!
Emblem of happiness,
Blest is thy dwelling-place--
Oh, to abide in the desert with thee!

JAMES HOGG

33. THE SANDPIPER

Across the lonely beach we flit,
One little sandpiper and I,
And fast I gather, bit by bit,
The scattered driftwood, bleached and dry.
The wild waves reach their hands for it,
The wild wind raves, the tide runs high,
As up and down the beach we flit,
One little sandpiper and I.

Above our heads the sullen clouds
Scud, black and swift, across the sky;
Like silent ghosts in misty shrouds
Stand out the white lighthouses high.
Almost as far as eye can reach
I see the close-reefed vessels fly,
As fast we flit along the beach,
One little sandpiper and I.

I watch him as he skims along,
Uttering his sweet and mournful cry;
He starts not at my fitful song,
Nor flash of fluttering drapery.
He has no thought of any wrong,
He scans me with a fearless eye;
Stanch friends are we, well tried and strong,
The little sandpiper and I.

Comrade, where wilt thou be to-night,
When the loosed storm breaks furiously?
My driftwood fire will burn so bright!
To what warm shelter canst thou fly?
I do not fear for thee, though wroth
The tempest rushes through the sky;
For are we not God's children both,
Thou, little sandpiper, and I?

CELIA THAXTER

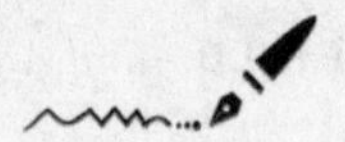

34. THE OWL

When cats run home and light is come,
And dew is cold upon the ground,
And the far-off stream is dumb,
And the whirring sail goes round,
And the whirring sail goes round;
Alone and warming his five wits,
The white owl in the belfry sits.

When merry milkmaids click the latch,
And rarely smells the new-mown hay,
And the cock hath sung beneath the thatch
Twice or thrice his roundelay,
Twice or thrice his roundelay;
Alone and warming his five wits,
The white owl in the belfry sits.

ALFRED TENNYSON

35. THE FLYING SQUIRREL
(A FRAGMENT)

Of all the woodland creatures,
The quaintest little sprite
Is the dainty flying squirrel
In vest of shining white,
In coat of silver gray,
And vest of shining white.

His furry Quaker jacket
Is trimmed with stripe of black;
A furry plume to match it
Is curling o'er his back;
New curved with every motion,
His plume curls o'er his back.

No little new-born baby
Has pinker feet than he;
Each tiny toe is cushioned
With velvet cushions three;
Three wee, pink, velvet cushions
Almost too small to see.

Who said, "The foot of baby
Might tempt an angel's kiss"?
I know a score of school-boys
Who put their lips to this,--
This wee foot of the squirrel,
And left a loving kiss.

(...)

MARY E. BURT

36. THE NIGHTINGALE AND THE GLOW-WORM

A nightingale, that all day long
Had cheered the village with his song,
Nor yet at eve his note suspended,
Nor yet when eventide was ended,
Began to feel, as well he might,
The keen demands of appetite;

When, looking eagerly around,
He spied far off, upon the ground,
A something shining in the dark,
And knew the glow-worm by his spark;
So, stooping down from hawthorn top,
He thought to put him in his crop.

The worm, aware of his intent,
Harangued him thus, right eloquent:
"Did you admire my lamp," quoth he,
"As much as I your minstrelsy,
You would abhor to do me wrong,
As much as I to spoil your song;

For 'twas the self-same power divine,
Taught you to sing and me to shine;
That you with music, I with light,
Might beautify and cheer the night."

The songster heard his short oration,
And warbling out his approbation,
Released him, as my story tells,
And found a supper somewhere else.

WILLIAM COWPER

37. THE BUTTERFLY AND THE BEE

Methought I heard a butterfly
Say to a labouring bee:
"Thou hast no colours of the sky
On painted wings like me."

"Poor child of vanity! those dyes,
And colours bright and rare,"
With mild reproof, the bee replies,
"Are all beneath my care.

"Content I toil from morn to eve,
And scorning idleness,
To tribes of gaudy sloth I leave
The vanity of dress."

WILLIAM LISLE BOWLES

38. A CHRYSALIS

My little Mädchen found one day
A curious something in her play,
That was not fruit, nor flower, nor seed;
It was not anything that grew,
Or crept, or climbed, or swam, or flew;
Had neither legs nor wings, indeed;
And yet she was not sure, she said,
Whether it was alive or dead.

She brought it in her tiny hand
To see if I would understand,
And wondered when I made reply,
"You've found a baby butterfly."
"A butterfly is not like this,"
With doubtful look she answered me.
So then I told her what would be
Some day within the chrysalis:
How, slowly, in the dull brown thing
Now still as death, a spotted wing,
And then another, would unfold,
Till from the empty shell would fly
A pretty creature, by and by,
All radiant in blue and gold.

"And will it, truly?" questioned she--
Her laughing lips and eager eyes
All in a sparkle of surprise--
"And shall your little Mädchen see?"
"She shall!" I said. How could I tell
That ere the worm within its shell
Its gauzy, splendid wings had spread,
My little Mädchen would be dead?

To-day the butterfly has flown,--
She was not here to see it fly,--
And sorrowing I wonder why
The empty shell is mine alone.
Perhaps the secret lies in this:
I too had found a chrysalis,
And Death that robbed me of delight
Was but the radiant creature's flight!

MARY EMILY BRADLEY

39. THE NAUTILUS AND THE AMMONITE

The nautilus and the ammonite
Were launched in friendly strife,
Each sent to float in its tiny boat
On the wide, wide sea of life.

For each could swim on the ocean's brim,
And, when wearied, its sail could furl,
And sink to sleep in the great sea-deep,
In its palace all of pearl.

And theirs was a bliss more fair than this
Which we taste in our colder clime;
For they were rife in a tropic life--
A brighter and better clime.

They swam 'mid isles whose summer smiles
Were dimmed by no alloy;
Whose groves were palm, whose air was balm,
And life one only joy.

They sailed all day through creek and bay,
And traversed the ocean deep;
And at night they sank on a coral bank,
In its fairy bowers to sleep.

And the monsters vast of ages past
They beheld in their ocean caves;
They saw them ride in their power and pride,
And sink in their deep-sea graves.

And hand in hand, from strand to strand,
They sailed in mirth and glee;
These fairy shells, with their crystal cells,
Twin sisters of the sea.

And they came at last to a sea long past,
But as they reached its shore,
The Almighty's breath spoke out in death,
And the ammonite was no more.

So the nautilus now in its shelly prow,
As over the deep it strays,
Still seems to seek, in bay and creek,
Its companion of other days.

And alike do we, on life's stormy sea,
As we roam from shore to shore,
Thus tempest-tossed, seek the loved, the lost,
And find them on earth no more.

Yet the hope how sweet, again to meet,
As we look to a distant strand,
Where heart meets heart, and no more they part
Who meet in that better land.

ANONYMOUS

40. THE DUEL

The gingham dog and the calico cat
Side by side on the table sat;
'Twas half-past twelve, and (what do you think!)
Nor one nor t'other had slept a wink!
The old Dutch clock and the Chinese plate
Appeared to know as sure as fate
There was going to be a terrible spat.
(_I wasn't there; I simply state
What was told to me by the Chinese plate_!)

The gingham dog went "bow-wow-wow!"
And the calico cat replied "mee-ow!"
The air was littered, an hour or so,
With bits of gingham and calico,
While the old Dutch clock in the chimney-place
Up with its hands before its face,
For it always dreaded a family row!
(_Now mind: I'm only telling you
What the old Dutch clock declares is true_!)

The Chinese plate looked very blue,
And wailed, "Oh, dear! what shall we do!"
But the gingham dog and the calico cat
Wallowed this way and tumbled that,
Employing every tooth and claw
In the awfullest way you ever saw--
And, oh! how the gingham and calico flew!
(_Don't fancy I exaggerate!
I got my views from the Chinese plate_!)

Next morning where the two had sat
They found no trace of the dog or cat;
And some folks think unto this day
That burglars stole the pair away!
But the truth about the cat and the pup
Is this: They ate each other up!
Now what do you really think of that!
(_The old Dutch clock it told me so,
And that is how I came to know_.)

EUGENE FIELD

41. PLAYING ROBINSON CRUSOE

Pussy can sit by the fire and sing,
Pussy can climb a tree,
Or play with a silly old cork and string
To 'muse herself, not me.
But I like Binkie, my dog, because
He knows how to behave;
So, Binkie's the same as the First Friend was,
And I am the Man in the Cave.

Pussy will play Man-Friday till
It's time to wet her paw
And make her walk on the window-sill
(For the footprint Crusoe saw);
Then she fluffles her tail and mews,
And scratches and won't attend.
But Binkie will play whatever I choose,
And he is my true First Friend.

Pussy will rub my knees with her head,
Pretending she loves me hard;
But the very minute I go to my bed
Pussy runs out in the yard.

And there she stays till the morning light;
So I know it is only pretend;
But Binkie, he snores at my feet all night,
And he is my Firstest Friend!

RUDYARD KIPLING

42. LET DOGS DELIGHT TO BARK AND BITE

Let dogs delight to bark and bite,
For God hath made them so;
Let bears and lions growl and fight,
For 'tis their nature too.

But, children, you should never let
Such angry passions rise;
Your little hands were never made
To tear each other's eyes.

ISAAC WATTS

43. FAIRY SONG

Shed no tear! O shed no tear!
The flower will bloom another year.
Weep no more! O, weep no more!
Young buds sleep in the root's white core.
Dry your eyes! Oh! dry your eyes!
For I was taught in Paradise
To ease my breast of melodies--
    Shed no tear.

Overhead! look overhead!
'Mong the blossoms white and red--
Look up, look up. I flutter now
On this flush pomegranate bough.
See me! 'tis this silvery bell
Ever cures the good man's ill.
Shed no tear! O, shed no tear!
The flowers will bloom another year.
Adieu, adieu--I fly, adieu,
I vanish in the heaven's blue--
    Adieu, adieu!

JOHN KEATS

IV

OF SIMPLE THINGS

44. LITTLE THINGS

Little drops of water,
Little grains of sand,
Make the mighty ocean
And the pleasant land.

Thus the little minutes,
Humble though they be,
Make the mighty ages
Of eternity.

EBENEZER COBHAM BREWER

45. THE DAYS OF THE MONTH

Thirty days hath September,
April, June, and November;
February has twenty-eight alone.
All the rest have thirty-one,
Excepting leap-year--that's the time
When February's days are twenty-nine.

OLD SONG

46. THE ARROW AND THE SONG

I shot an arrow into the air,
It fell to earth, I knew not where;
For, so swiftly it flew, the sight
Could not follow it in its flight.

I breathed a song into the air,
It fell to earth, I knew not where;
For who has sight so keen and strong
That it can follow the flight of song?

Long, long afterward, in an oak
I found the arrow, still unbroke;
And the song, from beginning to end,
I found again in the heart of a friend.

HENRY W. LONGFELLOW

47. THE OLD OAKEN BUCKET

How dear to this heart are the scenes of my childhood,
When fond recollection presents them to view!
The orchard, the meadow, the deep-tangled wild-wood,
And every loved spot which my infancy knew!
The wide-spreading pond, and the mill that stood by it,
The bridge, and the rock where the cataract fell,
The cot of my father, the dairy-house nigh it,
And e'en the rude bucket that hung in the well--
The old oaken bucket, the iron-bound bucket,
The moss-covered bucket which hung in the well.

That moss-covered vessel I hailed as a treasure,
For often at noon, when returned from the field,
I found it the source of an exquisite pleasure,
The purest and sweetest that nature can yield.
How ardent I seized it, with hands that were glowing,
And quick to the white-pebbled bottom it fell;
Then soon, with the emblem of truth overflowing,
And dripping with coolness, it rose from the well--
The old oaken bucket, the iron-bound bucket,
The moss-covered bucket arose from the well.

How sweet from the green mossy brim to receive it
As poised on the curb it inclined to my lips!
Not a full blushing goblet could tempt me to leave it,
The brightest that beauty or revelry sips.
And now, far removed from the loved habitation,
The tear of regret will intrusively swell.
As fancy reverts to my father's plantation,
And sighs for the bucket that hangs in the well--
The old oaken bucket, the iron-bound bucket,
The moss-covered bucket that hangs in the well!

SAMUEL WOODWORTH

48. LETTY'S GLOBE

When Letty had scarce pass'd her third glad year,
And her young, artless words began to flow,
One day we gave the child a colour'd sphere
Of the wide earth, that she might mark and know,
By tint and outline, all its sea and land.
She patted all the world; old empires peep'd
Between her baby fingers; her soft hand
Was welcome at all frontiers. How she leap'd,
And laugh'd and prattled in her world-wide bliss!
But when we turn'd her sweet unlearned eye
On our own isle, she rais'd a joyous cry,
"Oh! yes, I see it! Letty's home is there!"
And, while she hid all England with a kiss,
Bright over Europe fell her golden hair!

CHARLES TENNYSON TURNER

49. HOME, SWEET HOME!

'Mid pleasures and palaces though we may roam,
Be it ever so humble, there's no place like home;
A charm from the sky seems to hallow us there,
Which, seek through the world, is ne'er met with elsewhere.
    Home! Home! sweet, sweet Home!
There's no place like Home! there's no place like Home!

An exile from Home, splendour dazzles in vain;
O, give me my lowly thatched cottage again!
The birds singing gaily, that came at my call,--
Give me them,--and the peace of mind, dearer than all!
    Home! Home! sweet, sweet Home!
There's no place like Home! there's no place like Home!

How sweet 'tis to sit 'neath a fond father's smile,
And the cares of a mother to soothe and beguile!
Let others delight 'mid new pleasures to roam,
But give me, oh, give me, the pleasures of Home!
    Home! Home! sweet, sweet Home!
There's no place like Home! there's no place like Home!

To thee I'll return, overburdened with care;
The heart's dearest solace will smile on me there;
No more from that cottage again will I roam;
Be it ever so humble, there's no place like Home.
    Home! Home! sweet, sweet Home!
There's no place like Home! there's no place like Home!

JOHN HOWARD PAYNE

50. MY SHADOW

I have a little shadow that goes in and out with me,
And what can be the use of him is more than I can see.
He is very, very like me from the heels up to the head;
And I see him jump before me, when I jump into my bed.

The funniest thing about him is the way he likes to grow--
Not at all like proper children, which is always very slow;
For he sometimes shoots up taller like an india-rubber ball,
And he sometimes gets so little that there's none of him at all.

He hasn't got a notion of how children ought to play,
And can only make a fool of me in every sort of way.
He stays so close beside me, he's a coward, you can see;
I'd think shame to stick to nursie as that shadow sticks to me!

One morning, very early, before the sun was up,
I rose and found the shining dew on every buttercup;
But my lazy little shadow, like an arrant sleepy-head,
Had stayed at home behind me and was fast asleep in bed.

ROBERT LOUIS STEVENSON

51. A MUSICAL INSTRUMENT

What was he doing, the great god Pan,
Down in the reeds by the river?
Spreading ruin and scattering ban,
Splashing and paddling with hoofs of a goat,
And breaking the golden lilies afloat
With the dragon-fly on the river.

He tore out a reed, the great god Pan,
From the deep cool bed of the river:
The limpid water turbidly ran,
And the broken lilies a-dying lay,
And the dragon-fly had fled away,
Ere he brought it out of the river.

High on the shore sat the great god Pan,
While turbidly flow'd the river;
And hack'd and hew'd as a great god can,
With his hard bleak steel at the patient reed,
Till there was not a sign of a leaf indeed
To prove it fresh from the river.

He cut it short, did the great god Pan
(How tall it stood in the river!),
Then drew the pith, like the heart of a man,
Steadily from the outside ring,
And notched the poor dry empty thing
In holes, as he sat by the river.

"This is the way," laugh'd the great god Pan
(Laugh'd while he sat by the river),
"The only way, since gods began
To make sweet music, they could succeed."
Then, dropping his mouth to a hole in the reed
He blew in power by the river.

Sweet, sweet, sweet, O Pan!
Piercing sweet by the river!
Blinding sweet, O great god Pan!
The sun on the hill forgot to die,
And the lilies reviv'd, and the dragon-fly
Came back to dream on the river.

Yet half a beast is the great god Pan,
To laugh as he sits by the river,
Making a poet out of a man:
The true gods sigh for the cost and pain,--
For the reed which grows nevermore again
As a reed with the reeds in the river.

ELIZABETH BARRETT BROWNING

52. THE HARP THAT ONCE THROUGH TARA'S HALLS

The harp that once through Tara's halls
The soul of music shed,
Now hangs as mute on Tara's walls
As if that soul were fled.
So sleeps the pride of former days,
So glory's thrill is o'er,
And hearts, that once beat high for praise,
Now feel that pulse no more.

No more to chiefs and ladies bright
The harp of Tara swells;
The chord alone, that breaks at night,
Its tale of ruin tells.
Thus Freedom now so seldom wakes,
The only throb she gives
Is when some heart indignant breaks,
To show that still she lives.

THOMAS MOORE

53. THE FINDING OF THE LYRE

There lay upon the ocean's shore
What once a tortoise served to cover;
A year and more, with rush and roar,
The surf had rolled it over,
Had played with it, and flung it by,
As wind and weather might decide it,
Then tossed it high where sand-drifts dry
Cheap burial might provide it.

It rested there to bleach or tan,
The rains had soaked, the sun had burned it;
With many a ban the fisherman
Had stumbled o'er and spurned it;
And there the fisher-girl would stay,
Conjecturing with her brother
How in their play the poor estray
Might serve some use or other.

So there it lay, through wet and dry,
As empty as the last new sonnet,
Till by and by came Mercury,
And, having mused upon it,
"Why, here," cried he, "the thing of things
In shape, material, and dimension!
Give it but strings, and, lo, it sings,
A wonderful invention!"

So said, so done; the chords he strained,
And, as his fingers o'er them hovered,
The shell disdained a soul had gained,
The lyre had been discovered.
O empty world that round us lies,
Dead shell, of soul and thought forsaken,
Brought we but eyes like Mercury's,
In thee what songs should waken!

JAMES RUSSELL LOWELL

54. THE BUGLE SONG

The splendour falls on castle walls
And snowy summits old in story:
The long light shakes across the lakes
And the wild cataract leaps in glory.
Blow, bugle, blow, set the wild echoes flying,
Blow, bugle; answer, echoes, dying, dying, dying.

O hark, O hear! how thin and clear,
And thinner, clearer, farther going!
O sweet and far from cliff and scar
The horns of Elfland faintly blowing!
Blow, let us hear the purple glens replying:
Blow, bugle; answer, echoes, dying, dying, dying.

O love, they die in yon rich sky,
They faint on hill or field or river:
Our echoes roll from soul to soul,
And grow forever and forever.
Blow, bugle, blow, set the wild echoes flying,
And answer, echoes, answer, dying, dying, dying.

ALFRED TENNYSON

55. MY TYPEWRITER

I have a trim typewriter now,
They tell me none is better;
It makes a pleasing, rhythmic row,
And neat is every letter.
I tick out stories by machine,
Dig pars, and gags, and verses keen,
And lathe them off in manner slick.
It is so easy, and it's quick.

And yet it falls short, I'm afraid,
Of giving satisfaction,
This making literature by aid
Of scientific traction;
For often, I can't fail to see,
The dashed thing runs away with me.
It bolts, and do whate'er I may
I cannot hold the runaway.

It is not fitted with a brake,
And endless are my verses,
Nor any yarn I start to make
Appropriately terse is.
'Tis plain that this machine-made screed
Is fit but for machines to read;
So "Wanted" (as an iron censor)
"A good, sound, secondhand condenser"!

EDWARD DYSON

56. A BOOK

There is no frigate like a book
To take us lands away,
Nor any coursers like a page
Of prancing poetry.
This traverse may the poorest take
Without oppress of toll;
How frugal is the chariot
That bears a human soul!

EMILY ELIZABETH DICKINSON

57. A WORD

A word is dead
When it is said,
Some say.
I say it just
Begins to live
That day.

EMILY ELIZABETH DICKINSON

V

OF COMMON PEOPLE
AND NOT SO COMMON VIRTUES

58. THE BOY WHO NEVER TOLD A LIE

Once there was a little boy,
With curly hair and pleasant eye--
A boy who always told the truth,
And never, never told a lie.

And when he trotted off to school,
The children all about would cry,
"There goes the curly-headed boy--
The boy that never tells a lie."

And everybody loved him so,
Because he always told the truth,
That every day, as he grew up,
'Twas said, "There goes the honest youth."

And when the people that stood near
Would turn to ask the reason why,
The answer would be always this:
"Because he never tells a lie."

ANONYMOUS

59. CONTENTMENT

My mind to me a kingdom is;
Such perfect joy therein I find
As far excels all earthly bliss
That God or Nature hath assigned;
Though much I want that most would have,
Yet still my mind forbids to crave.

Content I live; this is my stay,--
I seek no more than may suffice.
I press to bear no haughty sway;
Look, what I lack my mind supplies.
Lo, thus I triumph like a king,
Content with that my mind doth bring.

I laugh not at another's loss,
I grudge not at another's gain;
No worldly wave my mind can toss;
I brook that is another's bane.
I fear no foe, nor fawn on friend;
I loathe not life, nor dread mine end.

My wealth is health and perfect ease;
My conscience clear my chief defense;
I never seek by bribes to please
Nor by desert to give offense.
Thus do I live, thus will I die;
Would all did so as well as I!

EDWARD DYER

60. SOLITUDE

Happy the man, whose wish and care
A few paternal acres bound,
Content to breathe his native air
In his own ground.

Whose herds with milk, whose fields with bread,
Whose flocks supply him with attire;
Whose trees in summer yield him shade,
In winter fire.

Blest, who can unconcern'dly find
Hours, days, and years slide soft away
In health of body, peace of mind,
Quiet by day,

Sound sleep by night; study and ease
Together mixt, sweet recreation,
And innocence, which most does please
With meditation.

Thus let me live, unseen, unknown;
Thus unlamented let me die;
Steal from the world, and not a stone
Tell where I lie.

ALEXANDER POPE

61. IF...

If you can keep your head when all about you
Are losing theirs and blaming it on you;
If you can trust yourself when all men doubt you,
But make allowance for their doubting too;
If you can wait and not be tired by waiting,
Or being lied about, don't deal in lies,
Or being hated, don't give way to hating,
And yet don't look too good, nor talk too wise:

If you can dream, and not make dreams your master;
If you can think, and not make thoughts your aim;
If you can meet with Triumph and Disaster
And treat those two imposters just the same;
If you can bear to hear the truth you've spoken
Twisted by knaves to make a trap for fools,
Or watch the things you gave your life to, broken,
And stoop and build 'em up with worn-out tools;

If you can make one heap of all your winnings
And risk it on one turn of pitch-and-toss,
And lose, and start again at your beginnings
And never breathe a word about your loss;
If you can force your heart and nerve and sinew
To serve your turn long after they are gone,
And so hold on when there is nothing in you
Except the Will which says to them: "Hold on!"

If you can talk with crowds and keep your virtue,
Or walk with kings, nor lose the common touch,
If neither foes nor loving friends can hurt you,
If all men count with you, but none too much;
If you can fill the unforgiving minute
With sixty seconds' worth of distance run,
Yours is the Earth and everything that's in it,
And, which is more, you'll be a Man, my son!

RUDYARD KIPLING

62. MOTHER O' MINE

If I were hanged on the highest hill,
    Mother o' mine, O mother o' mine!
I know whose love would follow me still,
    Mother o' mine, O mother o' mine!

If I were drowned in the deepest sea,
    Mother o' mine, O mother o' mine!
I know whose tears would come down to me,
    Mother o' mine, O mother o' mine!

If I were damned of body and soul,
I know whose prayers would make me whole,
    Mother o' mine, O mother o' mine!

RUDYARD KIPLING

63. MY FATHER'S CHAIR

There are four good legs to my Father's Chair,
Priests and People and Lords and Crown.
I sits on all of 'em fair and square,
And that is reason it don't break down.

I won't trust one leg, nor two, nor three,
To carry my weight when I sets me down.
I wants all four of 'em under me,
Priests and People and Lords and Crown.

I sits on all four and favours none,
Priests, nor People, nor Lords, nor Crown:
And I never tilts in my chair, my son,
And that is the reason it don't break down.

When your time comes to sit in my Chair,
Remember your Father's habits and rules,
Sit on all four legs, fair and square,
And never be tempted by one-legged stools!

RUDYARD KIPLING

64. FATHER WILLIAM

"You are old, Father William," the young man said,
"And your hair has become very white;
And yet you incessantly stand on your head--
Do you think, at your age, it is right?"

"In my youth," Father William replied to his son,
"I feared it might injure the brain;
But now that I'm perfectly sure I have none,
Why, I do it again and again."

"You are old," said the youth, "as I mentioned before,
And have grown most uncommonly fat;
Yet you turned a back-somersault in at the door--
Pray, what is the reason of that?"

"In my youth," said the sage, as he shook his gray locks,
"I kept all my limbs very supple
By the use of this ointment--one shilling the box--
Allow me to sell you a couple."

"You are old," said the youth, "and your jaws are too weak
For anything tougher than suet;
Yet you finished the goose, with the bones and the beak:
Pray, how did you manage to do it?"

"In my youth," said his father, "I took to the law,
And argued each case with my wife;
And the muscular strength which it gave to my jaw
Has lasted the rest of my life."

"You are old," said the youth; "one would hardly suppose
That your eye was as steady as ever;
Yet you balanced an eel on the end of your nose--
What made you so awfully clever?"

"I have answered three questions, and that is enough,"
Said his father, "don't give yourself airs!
Do you think I can listen all day to such stuff?
Be off, or I'll kick you down-stairs!"

LEWIS CARROLL

65. THE VILLAGE BLACKSMITH
(A FRAGMENT)

Under a spreading chestnut-tree
The village smithy stands;
The smith, a mighty man is he,
With large and sinewy hands,
And the muscles of his brawny arms
Are strong as iron bands.

His hair is crisp, and black, and long;
His face is like the tan;
His brow is wet with honest sweat,
He earns whate'er he can,
And looks the whole world in the face,
For he owes not any man.

Week in, week out, from morn till night,
You can hear his bellows blow;
You can hear him swing his heavy sledge,
With measured beat and slow,
Like a sexton ringing the village bell,
When the evening sun is low.

And children coming home from school
Look in at the open door;
They love to see the flaming forge,
And hear the bellows roar,
And catch the burning sparks that fly
Like chaff from a threshing-floor.

(...)

Thanks, thanks to thee, my worthy friend,
For the lesson thou hast taught!
Thus at the flaming forge of life
Our fortunes must be wrought;
Thus on its sounding anvil shaped
Each burning deed and thought.

HENRY W. LONGFELLOW

66. ABOU BEN ADHEM

Abou Ben Adhem (may his tribe increase!)
Awoke one night from a deep dream of peace,
And saw within the moonlight in his room,
Making it rich and like a lily in bloom,
An angel writing in a book of gold.

Exceeding peace had made Ben Adhem bold;
And to the presence in the room he said,
"What writest thou?" The vision raised its head,
And, with a look made of all sweet accord,
Answered, "The names of those who love the Lord."

"And is mine one?" said Abou. "Nay, not so,"
Replied the angel. Abou spoke more low,
But cheerly still; and said, "I pray thee, then,
Write me as one that loves his fellow-men."

The angel wrote, and vanished. The next night
It came again, with a great wakening light,
And showed the names whom love of God had blessed;
And, lo! Ben Adhem's name led all the rest.

LEIGH HUNT

67. JOHN ANDERSON

John Anderson, my jo, John,
When we were first acquent
Your locks were like the raven,
Your bonnie brow was brent;
But now your brow is bald, John,
Your locks are like the snow;
But blessings on your frosty pow,
John Anderson, my jo.

John Anderson, my jo, John,
We clamb the hill thegither,
And mony a canty day, John,
We've had wi' ane anither;
Now we maun totter down, John,
But hand in hand we'll go,
And sleep thegither at the foot,
John Anderson, my jo.

ROBERT BURNS

VI

OF REAL ADVENTURES
AND NOT SO REAL TALES

68. SOON MAY THE WELLERMAN COME

There was a ship that put to sea,
The name of the ship was the Billy of Tea
The winds blew up, her bow dipped down,
O blow, my bully boys, blow.

Soon may the Wellerman come
And bring us sugar and tea and rum.
One day, when the tonguin' is done,
We'll take our leave and go.

She had not been two weeks from shore
When down on her a right whale bore.
The captain called all hands and swore
He'd take that whale in tow.

Before the boat had hit the water
The whale's tail came up and caught her.
All hands to the side, harpooned and fought her
When she dived down below.

No line was cut, no whale was freed;
The Captain's mind was not of greed,
But he belonged to the whaleman's creed;
She took the ship in tow.

For forty days, or even more,
The line went slack, then tight once more.
All boats were lost (there were only four)
But still the whale did go.

As far as I know, the fight's still on;
The line's not cut and the whale's not gone.
The Wellerman makes his regular call
To the Captain, crew, and all.

ANONYMOUS NEW ZEALAND FOLK SONG

69. A LIFE ON THE OCEAN WAVE

A life on the ocean wave,
A home on the rolling deep,
Where the scattered waters rave,
And the winds their revels keep!
Like an eagle caged, I pine
On this dull, unchanging shore:
Oh! give me the flashing brine,
The spray and the tempest's roar!

Once more on the deck I stand
Of my own swift-gliding craft:
Set sail! farewell to the land!
The gale follows fair abaft.
We shoot through the sparkling foam
Like an ocean-bird set free;--
Like the ocean-bird, our home
We'll find far out on the sea.

The land is no longer in view,
The clouds have begun to frown;
But with a stout vessel and crew,
We'll say, Let the storm come down!
And the song of our hearts shall be,
While the winds and the waters rave,
A home on the rolling sea!
A life on the ocean wave!

EPES SARGENT

70. SWEET AND LOW

Sweet and low, sweet and low,
Wind of the western sea,
Low, low, breathe and blow,
Wind of the western sea!
Over the rolling waters go,
Come from the dropping moon and blow,
Blow him again to me;
While my little one, while my pretty one sleeps.

Sleep and rest, sleep and rest,
Father will come to thee soon;
Rest, rest, on mother's breast,
Father will come to thee soon;
Father will come to his babe in the nest,
Silver sails all out of the west
Under the silver moon:
Sleep, my little one, sleep, my pretty one, sleep.

ALFRED TENNYSON

71. THE "THREE BELLS" OF GLASGOW

Beneath the low-hung night cloud
That raked her splintering mast
The good ship settled slowly,
The cruel leak gained fast.

Over the awful ocean
Her signal guns pealed out.
Dear God! was that Thy answer
From the horror round about?

A voice came down the wild wind,
"Ho! ship ahoy!" its cry:
"Our stout _Three Bells_ of Glasgow
Shall stand till daylight by!"

Hour after hour crept slowly,
Yet on the heaving swells
Tossed up and down the ship-lights,
The lights of the _Three Bells_!

And ship to ship made signals,
Man answered back to man,
While oft, to cheer and hearten,
The _Three Bells_ nearer ran:

And the captain from her taffrail
Sent down his hopeful cry.
"Take heart! Hold on!" he shouted,
"The _Three Bells_ shall stand by!"

All night across the waters
The tossing lights shone clear;
All night from reeling taffrail
The _Three Bells_ sent her cheer.

And when the dreary watches
Of storm and darkness passed,
Just as the wreck lurched under,
All souls were saved at last.

Sail on, _Three Bells_, forever,
In grateful memory sail!
Ring on, _Three Bells_ of rescue,
Above the wave and gale!

Type of the Love eternal,
Repeat the Master's cry,
As tossing through our darkness
The lights of God draw nigh!

JOHN G. WHITTIER

72. TRUE ROYALTY

There was never a Queen like Balkis,
From here to the wide world's end;
But Balkis talked to a butterfly
As you would talk to a friend.

There was never a King like Solomon,
Not since the world began;
But Solomon talked to a butterfly
As a man would talk to a man.

She was Queen of Sabaea--
And _he_ was Asia's Lord--
But they both of 'em talked to butterflies
When they took their walks abroad.

RUDYARD KIPLING

73. A BALLAD OF THE TWO KINGS

Two knights rode forth at early dawn
A-seeking maids to wed,
Said one, "My lady must be fair,
With gold hair on her head."

Then spake the other knight-at-arms:
"I care not for her face,
But she I love must be a dove
For purity and grace."

And each knight blew upon his horn
And went his separate way,
And each knight found a lady-love
Before the fall of day.

But she was brown who should have had
The shining yellow hair,
I ween the knights forgot their words
Or else they ceased to care.

For he who wanted purity
Brought home a wanton wild,
And when each saw the other knight
I seen that each knight smiled.

SARA TEASDALE

74. THE GLOVE AND THE LIONS

King Francis was a hearty king, and loved a royal sport,
And one day as his lions fought, sat looking on the court;
The nobles filled the benches, with the ladies in their pride,
And 'mong them sat the Count de Lorge
          with one for whom he sighed:
And truly 'twas a gallant thing to see that crowning show,
Valour, and love, and a king above, and the royal beasts below.

Ramp'd and roar'd the lions, with horrid laughing jaws;
They bit, they glared, gave blows like beams,
          a wind went with their paws;
With wallowing might and stifled roar they rolled on one another,
Till all the pit with sand and mane was in a thunderous smother;
The bloody foam above the bars came whisking through the air;
Said Francis then, "Faith, gentlemen, we're better here than there."

De Lorge's love o'erheard the King,--a beauteous lively dame
With smiling lips and sharp, bright eyes,
          which always seem'd the same:
She thought, "The Count, my lover, is brave as brave can be;
He surely would do wondrous things to show his love of me;
King, ladies, lovers, all look on; the occasion is divine;
I'll drop my glove, to prove his love; great glory will be mine."

She dropped her glove, to prove his love,
          then look'dat him and smiled;
He bowed, and in a moment leapt among the lions wild:
His leap was quick, return was quick, he has regain'd his place,
Then threw the glove, but not with love, right in the lady's face.
"Well done!" cried Francis, "bravely done!"
          and he rose from where he sat:
"No love," quoth he, "but vanity, sets love a task like that."

LEIGH HUNT

75. A BALLAD FOR A BOY
(A FRAGMENT)

When George the Third was reigning, a hundred years ago,
He ordered Captain Farmer to chase the foreign foe,
"You're not afraid of shot," said he, "you're not afraid of wreck,
So cruise about the west of France in the frigate called _Quebec_.

"Quebec was once a Frenchman's town, but twenty years ago
King George the Second sent a man called General Wolfe, you know,
To clamber up a precipice and look into Quebec,
As you'd look down a hatchway when standing on the deck.

"If Wolfe could beat the Frenchmen then, so you can beat them now.
Before he got inside the town he died, I must allow.
But since the town was won for us it is a lucky name,
And you'll remember Wolfe's good work and you shall do the same."

Then Farmer said, "I'll try, sir," and Farmer bowed so low
That George could see his pigtail tied in a velvet bow.
George gave him his commission, and that it might be safer,
Signed "King of Britain, King of France," and sealed it with a wafer.

(...)

VIOLO ROSEBORO

76. THE FLAG GOES BY

Hats off!
Along the street there comes
A blare of bugles, a ruffle of drums,
A flash of colour beneath the sky:
Hats off!
The flag is passing by!

Blue and crimson and white it shines
Over the steel-tipped, ordered lines.
Hats off!
The colours before us fly;
But more than the flag is passing by.

Sea-fights and land-fights, grim and great,
Fought to make and to save the State:
Weary marches and sinking ships;
Cheers of victory on dying lips;

Days of plenty and years of peace;
March of a strong land's swift increase;
Equal justice, right, and law,
Stately honour and reverend awe;

Sign of a nation, great and strong
Toward her people from foreign wrong:
Pride and glory and honour,--all
Live in the colours to stand or fall.

Hats off!
Along the street there comes
A blare of bugles, a ruffle of drums;
And loyal hearts are beating high:
Hats off!
The flag is passing by!

HENRY HOLCOMB BENNETT

77. THE HOMES OF ENGLAND
(A FRAGMENT)

The stately homes of England!
How beautiful they stand,
Amidst their tall ancestral trees,
O'er all the pleasant land!
The deer across their greensward bound
Through shade and sunny gleam,
And the swan glides past them with the sound
Of some rejoicing stream.

The merry homes of England!
Around their hearths by night
What gladsome looks of household love
Meet in the ruddy light!
There woman's voice flows forth in song,
Or childish tale is told,
Or lips move tunefully along
Some glorious page of old.

(...)

The free, fair homes of England!
Long, long, in hut and hall
May hearts of native proof be reared
To guard each hallowed wall!
And green forever be the groves,
And bright the flowery sod,
Where first the child's glad spirit loves
Its country and its God!

FELICIA HEMANS

78. THE SHEPHERD OF KING ADMETUS

There came a youth upon the earth,
Some thousand years ago,
Whose slender hands were nothing worth,
Whether to plow, or reap, or sow.

Upon an empty tortoise-shell
He stretched some chords, and drew
Music that made men's bosoms swell
Fearless, or brimmed their eyes with dew.

Then King Admetus, one who had
Pure taste by right divine,
Decreed his singing not too bad
To hear between the cups of wine:

And so, well pleased with being soothed
Into a sweet half-sleep,
Three times his kingly beard he smoothed,
And made him viceroy o'er his sheep.

His words were simple words enough,
And yet he used them so,
That what in other mouths was rough
In his seemed musical and low.

Men called him but a shiftless youth,
In whom no good they saw;
And yet, unwittingly, in truth,
They made his careless words their law.

They knew not how he learned at all,
For idly, hour by hour,
He sat and watched the dead leaves fall,
Or mused upon a common flower.

It seemed the loveliness of things
Did teach him all their use,
For, in mere weeds, and stones, and springs,
He found a healing power profuse.

Men granted that his speech was wise,
But, when a glance they caught
Of his slim grace and woman's eyes,
They laughed, and called him good-for-naught.

Yet after he was dead and gone,
And e'en his memory dim,
Earth seemed more sweet to live upon,
More full of love, because of him.

And day by day more holy grew
Each spot where he had trod,
Till after-poets only knew
Their first-born brother as a god.

JAMES RUSSELL LOWELL

79. COLUMBUS

Behind him lay the gray Azores,
Behind the gates of Hercules;
Before him not the ghost of shores,
Before him only shoreless seas.
The good mate said: "Now must we pray,
For lo! the very stars are gone;
Speak, Admiral, what shall I say?"
"Why say, sail on! and on!"

"My men grow mut'nous day by day;
My men grow ghastly wan and weak."
The stout mate thought of home; a spray
Of salt wave wash'd his swarthy cheek.
"What shall I say, brave Admiral,
If we sight naught but seas at dawn?"
"Why, you shall say, at break of day:
'Sail on! sail on! and on!'"

They sailed and sailed, as winds might blow,
Until at last the blanch'd mate said;
"Why, now, not even God would know
Should I and all my men fall dead.
These very winds forget their way,
For God from these dread seas is gone.
Now speak, brave Admiral, and say----"
He said: "Sail on! and on!"

They sailed, they sailed, then spoke his mate:
"This mad sea shows his teeth to-night,
He curls his lip, he lies in wait,
With lifted teeth as if to bite!
Brave Admiral, say but one word;
What shall we do when hope is gone?"
The words leaped as a leaping sword:
"Sail on! sail on! and on!"

Then, pale and worn, he kept his deck,
And thro' the darkness peered that night.
Ah, darkest night! and then a speck,--
A light! a light! a light! a light!
It grew--a star-lit flag unfurled!
It grew to be Time's burst of dawn;
He gained a world! he gave that world
Its watch-word: "On! and on!"

JOAQUIN MILLER

80. THE LANDING OF THE PILGRIMS

The breaking waves dashed high
On a stern and rock-bound coast,
And the woods against a stormy sky
Their giant branches tossed.

And the heavy night hung dark
The hills and waters o'er,
When a band of exiles moored their bark
On the wild New England shore.

Not as the conqueror comes,
They, the true-hearted, came;
Not with the roll of the stirring drums,
And the trumpet that sings of fame.

Not as the flying come,
In silence and in fear;
They shook the depths of the desert gloom
With their hymns of lofty cheer.

Amid the storm they sang,
And the stars heard, and the sea,
And the sounding aisles of the dim woods rang
To the anthem of the free!

The ocean eagle soared
From his nest by the white wave's foam;
And the rocking pines of the forest roared,--
This was their welcome home!

There were men with hoary hair,
Amid that pilgrim band;
Why had _they_ come to wither there,
Away from their childhood's land?

There was woman's fearless eye,
Lit by her deep love's truth;
There was manhood's brow serenely high,
And the fiery heart of youth.

What sought they thus afar?
Bright jewels of the mine?
The wealth of seas, the spoils of war?--
They sought a faith's pure shrine!

Ay! call it holy ground,
The soil where first they trod:
They have left unstained what there they found,
Freedom to worship God.

FELICIA HEMANS

81. THE SONG IN CAMP

"Give us a song!" the soldiers cried,
The outer trenches guarding,
When the heated guns of the camps allied
Grew weary of bombarding.

The dark Redan, in silent scoff,
Lay, grim and threatening, under;
And the tawny mound of the Malakoff
No longer belched its thunder.

There was a pause. A guardsman said,
"We storm the forts to-morrow;
Sing while we may, another day
Will bring enough of sorrow."

They lay along the battery's side,
Below the smoking cannon:
Brave hearts, from Severn and from Clyde,
And from the banks of Shannon.

They sang of love, and not of fame;
Forgot was Britain's glory:
Each heart recalled a different name,
But all sang "Annie Laurie."

Voice after voice caught up the song,
Until its tender passion
Rose like an anthem, rich and strong,--
Their battle-eve confession.

Dear girl, her name he dared not speak,
But, as the song grew louder,
Something upon the soldier's cheek
Washed off the stains of powder.

Beyond the darkening ocean burned
The bloody sunset's embers,
While the Crimean valleys learned
How English love remembers.

And once again a fire of hell
Rained on the Russian quarters,
With scream of shot, and burst of shell,
And bellowing of the mortars!

And Irish Nora's eyes are dim
For a singer, dumb and gory;
And English Mary mourns for him
Who sang of "Annie Laurie."

Sleep, soldiers! still in honoured rest
Your truth and valour wearing:
The bravest are the tenderest,--
The loving are the daring.

BAYARD TAYLOR

82. WYNKEN, BLYNKEN, AND NOD

Wynken, Blynken, and Nod one night
Sailed off in a wooden shoe,--
Sailed on a river of crystal light
Into a sea of dew.
"Where are you going, and what do you wish?"
The old moon asked the three.
"We have come to fish for the herring-fish
That live in this beautiful sea;
Nets of silver and gold have we,"
    Said Wynken,
    Blynken,
    And Nod.

The old moon laughed and sang a song,
As they rocked in the wooden shoe;
And the wind that sped them all night long
Ruffled the waves of dew;
The little stars were the herring-fish
That lived in the beautiful sea.
"Now cast your nets wherever you wish,--
Never afeard are we!"
So cried the stars to the fishermen three,
    Wynken,
    Blynken,
    And Nod.

All night long their nets they threw
To the stars in the twinkling foam,--
Then down from the skies came the wooden shoe,
Bringing the fishermen home:
'Twas all so pretty a sail, it seemed
As if it could not be;
And some folk thought 'twas a dream they'd dreamed
Of sailing that beautiful sea;
But I shall name you the fishermen three:
 Wynken,
 Blynken,
 And Nod.

Wynken and Blynken are two little eyes,
And Nod is a little head,
And the wooden shoe that sailed the skies
Is a wee one's trundle-bed;
So shut your eyes while Mother sings
Of wonderful sights that be,
And you shall see the beautiful things
As you rock on the misty sea
Where the old shoe rocked the fishermen three,
 Wynken,
 Blynken,
 And Nod.

EUGENE FIELD

83. THE WELL OF ST. KEYNE

A well there is in the west country,
And a clearer one never was seen;
There is not a wife in the west-country
But has heard of the Well of St. Keyne.

An oak and an elm tree stand beside,
And behind does an ash tree grow,
And a willow from the bank above
Droops to the water below.

A traveller came to the Well of St. Keyne:
Pleasant it was to his eye,
For from cock-crow he had been travelling
And there was not a cloud in the sky.

He drank of the water so cool and clear,
For thirsty and hot was he,
And he sat down upon the bank,
Under the willow tree.

There came a man from the neighbouring town
At the well to fill his pail;
On the well-side he rested it,
And bade the stranger hail.

"Now, art thou a bachelor, stranger?" quoth he,
"For an if thou hast a wife,
The happiest draught thou hast drunk this day
That ever thou didst in thy life.

"Or has your good woman, if one you have,
In Cornwall ever been?
For an if she have, I'll venture my life
She has drunk of the Well of St. Keyne."

"I have left a good woman who never was here,"
The stranger he made reply;
"But that my draught should be better for that,
I pray you answer me why,"

"St. Keyne," quoth the countryman, "many a time
Drank of this crystal well,
And before the angel summoned her
She laid on the water a spell.

"If the husband of this gifted well
Shall drink before his wife,
A happy man thenceforth is he,
For he shall be master for life.

"But if the wife should drink of it first,
God help the husband then!"
The stranger stoop'd to the Well of St. Keyne,
And drank of the waters again.

"You drank of the well, I warrant, betimes?"
He to the countryman said;
But the countryman smiled as the stranger spake,
And sheepishly shook his head.

"I hastened as soon as the wedding was done,
And left my wife in the porch,
But i' faith she had been wiser than me,
For she took a bottle to church,"

ROBERT SOUTHEY

84. LITTLE ORPHANT ANNIE

Little Orphant Annie's come to our house to stay,
An' wash the cups and saucers up, an' brush the crumbs away,
An' shoo the chickens off the porch, an' dust the hearth, an' sweep,
An' make the fire, an' bake the bread, an' earn her board-an'-keep;
An' all us other children, when the supper things is done,
We set around the kitchen fire an' has the mostest fun
A-list'nin' to the witch-tales 'at Annie tells about,
An' the Gobble-uns 'at gits you
      Ef you
         Don't
            Watch
            Out!

Onc't they was a little boy wouldn't say his pray'rs--
An' when he went to bed at night, away up-stairs,
His mammy heerd him holler, an' his daddy heerd him bawl,
An' when they turn't the kivvers down, he wasn't there at all!
An' they seeked him in the rafter-room, an' cubby hole, an' press,
An' seeked him up the chimbly flue, an' ever'-wheres, I guess;
But all they ever found was thist his pants an' roundabout!
An' the Gobble-uns'll git you
      Ef you
         Don't
            Watch
            Out!

An' one time a little girl 'ud allus laugh an' grin,
An' make fun of ever' one, an' all her blood-an'-kin;
An' onc't when they was "company," an' ole folks was there,
She mocked 'em an' shocked 'em, an' said she didn't care!
An' thist as she kicked her heels, an' turn't to run an' hide,
They was two great big Black Things a-standin' by her side,
An' they snatched her through the ceilin' 'fore she
                              knowed what she's about!
An' the Gobble-uns'll git you
          Ef you
              Don't
                  Watch
                  Out!

An' little Orphant Annie says, when the blaze is blue,
An' the lampwick sputters, an' the wind goes woo-oo!
An' you hear the crickets quit, an' the moon is gray,
An' the lightnin'-bugs in dew is all squenched away,--
You better mind yer parents, an' yer teachers fond an' dear,
An' churish them 'at loves you, an' dry the orphant's tear,
An' he'p the pore an' needy ones 'at clusters all about,
Er the Gobble-uns'll git you
          Ef you
              Don't
                  Watch
                  Out!

JAMES WHITCOMB RILEY

85. TWAS THE NIGHT BEFORE CHRISTMAS

'Twas the night before Christmas, when all through the house
Not a creature was stirring, not even a mouse;
The stockings were hung by the chimney with care,
In hopes that St. Nicholas soon would be there;

The children were nestled all snug in their beds,
While visions of sugar-plums danced in their heads;
And mamma in her 'kerchief, and I in my cap,
Had just settled our brains for a long winter's nap,

When out on the lawn there arose such a clatter,
I sprang from the bed to see what was the matter.
Away to the window I flew like a flash,
Tore open the shutters and threw up the sash.

The moon on the breast of the new-fallen snow
Gave the luster of mid-day to objects below,
When, what to my wondering eyes should appear,
But a miniature sleigh, and eight tiny reindeer.

With a little old driver, so lively and quick,
I knew in a moment it must be St. Nick.
More rapid than eagles his coursers they came,
And he whistled, and shouted, and called them by name:

"Now, _Dasher_! now, _Dancer_! now, _Prancer_ and _Vixen_!
On, _Comet_! on, _Cupid_! on, _Donder_ and _Blitzen_!
To the top of the porch! to the top of the wall!
Now dash away! dash away! dash away all!"

As dry leaves that before the wild hurricane fly,
When they meet with an obstacle, mount to the sky;
So up to the house-top the coursers they flew,
With the sleigh full of toys, and St. Nicholas, too.

And then, in a twinkling, I heard on the roof
The prancing and pawing of each little hoof.
As I drew in my head, and was turning around,
Down the chimney St. Nicholas came with a bound.

He was dressed all in fur, from his head to his foot,
And his clothes were all tarnished with ashes and soot;
A bundle of toys he had flung on his back,
And he looked like a peddler just opening his pack.

His eyes--how they twinkled! his dimples how merry!
His cheeks were like roses, his nose like a cherry!
His droll little mouth was drawn up like a bow,
And the beard of his chin was as white as the snow;

The stump of a pipe he held tight in his teeth,
And the smoke it encircled his head like a wreath;
He had a broad face and a little round belly,
That shook when he laughed, like a bowlful of jelly.

He was chubby and plump, a right jolly old elf,
And I laughed when I saw him, in spite of myself;
A wink of his eye and a twist of his head,
Soon gave me to know I had nothing to dread;

He spoke not a word, but went straight to his work,
And filled all the stockings; then turned with a jerk,
And laying his finger aside of his nose,
And giving a nod, up the chimney he rose;

He sprang to his sleigh, to his team gave a whistle,
And away they all flew like the down on a thistle.
But I heard him exclaim, ere he drove out of sight,
"_Happy Christmas to all, and to all a good-night_."

CLEMENT CLARKE MOORE

VII

OF FAITH, SADNESS, AND SORROW

86. MY OWN SHALL COME TO ME

Serene I fold my hands and wait,
Nor care for wind, nor tide, nor sea.
I rave no more 'gainst time or fate,
For lo! my own shall come to me.

I stay my haste, I make delays,
For what avails this eager pace?
I stand amid the eternal ways,
And what is mine shall know my face.

Asleep, awake, by night or day
The friends I seek are seeking me;
No wind can drive my bark astray,
Nor change the tide of destiny.

What matter if I stand alone?
I wait with joy the coming years;
My heart shall reap when it has sown,
And gather up its fruit of tears.

The stars come nightly to the sky;
The tidal wave comes to the sea;
Nor time, nor space, nor deep, nor high,
Can keep my own away from me.

The waters know their own and draw
The brook that springs in yonder heights;
So flows the good with equal law
Unto the soul of pure delights.

JOHN BURROUGHS

87. A NAME IN THE SAND

Alone I walked the ocean strand;
A pearly shell was in my hand:
I stooped and wrote upon the sand
My name--the year--the day.
As onward from the spot I passed,
One lingering look behind I cast;
A wave came rolling high and fast,
And washed my lines away.

And so, methought, 'twill shortly be
With every mark on earth from me:
A wave of dark oblivion's sea
Will sweep across the place
Where I have trod the sandy shore
Of time, and been, to be no more,
Of me--my day--the name I bore,
To leave nor track nor trace.

And yet, with Him who counts the sands
And holds the waters in His hands,
I know a lasting record stands
Inscribed against my name,
Of all this mortal part has wrought,
Of all this thinking soul has thought,
And from these fleeting moments caught
For glory or for shame.

HANNAH FLAGG GOULD

88. HOPE

Our lives, discoloured with our present woes,
May still grow white and shine with happier hours.
So the pure limped stream, when foul with stains
Of rushing torrents and descending rains,
Works itself clear, and as it runs refines,
till by degrees the floating mirror shines;
Reflects each flower that on the border grows,
And a new heaven in it's fair bosom shows.

JOSEPH ADDISON

89. THE THINGS WE DARE NOT TELL

The fields are fair in autumn yet,
    and the sun's still shining there,
But we bow our heads and we brood and fret,
    because of the masks we wear;
Or we nod and smile the social while,
    and we say we're doing well,
But we break our hearts, oh, we break our hearts!
    for the things we must not tell.

There's the old love wronged ere the new was won,
    there's the light of long ago;
There's the cruel lie that we suffer for,
    and the public must not know.
So we go through life with a ghastly mask,
    and we're doing fairly well,
While they break our hearts, oh, they kill our hearts!
    do the things we must not tell.

We see but pride in a selfish breast,
    while a heart is breaking there;
Oh, the world would be such a kindly world
    if all men's hearts lay bare!
We live and share the living lie,
    we are doing very well,
While they eat our hearts as the years go by,
    do the things we dare not tell.

We bow us down to a dusty shrine,
    or a temple in the East,
Or we stand and drink to the world-old creed,
    with the coffins at the feast;
We fight it down, and we live it down,
    or we bear it bravely well,
But the best men die of a broken heart
    for the things they cannot tell.

HENRY LAWSON

90. INGRATITUDE

Blow, blow, thou winter wind,
Thou are not so unkind
As man's ingratitude;
Thy tooth is not so keen
Because thou are not seen,
Although thy breath be rude.

Freeze, freeze, thou bitter sky,
Thou dost not bite so nigh
As benefits forgot;
Though thou the waters warp,
Thy sting is not so sharp
As friend remembered not.

WILLIAM SHAKESPEARE

91. A PSALM OF LIFE

Tell me not, in mournful numbers,
Life is but an empty dream!--
For the soul is dead that slumbers,
And things are not what they seem.

Life is real! Life is earnest!
And the grave is not its goal;
Dust thou art, to dust returnest,
Was not spoken of the soul.

Not enjoyment, and not sorrow,
Is our destined end or way;
But to act, that each to-morrow
Find us farther than to-day.

Art is long, and Time is fleeting,
And our hearts, though stout and brave,
Still, like muffled drums, are beating
Funeral marches to the grave.

In the world's broad field of battle,
In the bivouac of Life,
Be not like dumb, driven cattle!
Be a hero in the strife!

Trust no Future, howe'er pleasant!
Let the dead Past bury its dead!
Act,--act in the living Present!
Heart within, and God o'erhead!

Lives of great men all remind us
We can make our lives sublime,
And, departing, leave behind us
Footprints on the sands of time;

Footprints, that perhaps another,
Sailing o'er life's solemn main,
A forlorn and shipwrecked brother,
Seeing, shall take heart again.

Let us, then, be up and doing,
With a heart for any fate;
Still achieving, still pursuing,
Learn to labour and to wait.

HENRY W. LONGFELLOW

92. THE DEATH OF THE OLD YEAR

Full knee-deep lies the winter snow,
And the winter winds are wearily sighing:
Toll ye the church-bell sad and slow,
And tread softly and speak low,
For the old year lies a-dying.
   Old year, you must not die;
   You came to us so readily,
   You lived with us so steadily,
   Old year, you shall not die.

He lieth still: he doth not move:
He will not see the dawn of day.
He hath no other life above.
He gave me a friend, and a true true-love,
And the New-year will take 'em away.
   Old year, you must not go;
   So long as you have been with us,
   Such joy as you have seen with us,
   Old year, you shall not go.

He froth'd his bumpers to the brim;
A jollier year we shall not see.
But tho' his eyes are waxing dim,
And tho' his foes speak ill of him,
He was a friend to me.
   Old year, you shall not die;
   We did so laugh and cry with you,
   I've half a mind to die with you,
   Old year, if you must die.

He was full of joke and jest,
But all his merry quips are o'er.
To see him die, across the waste
His son and heir doth ride post-haste,
But he'll be dead before.
    Every one for his own.
    The night is starry and cold, my friend,
    And the New-year blithe and bold, my friend,
    Comes up to take his own.

How hard he breathes! over the snow
I heard just now the crowing cock.
The shadows flicker to and fro:
The cricket chirps: the light burns low:
'Tis nearly twelve o'clock.
    Shake hands, before you die.
    Old year, we'll dearly rue for you:
    What is it we can do for you?
    Speak out before you die.

His face is growing sharp and thin.
Alack! our friend is gone.
Close up his eyes: tie up his chin:
Step from the corpse, and let him in
That standeth there alone,
    And waiteth at the door.
    There's a new foot on the floor, my friend,
    And a new face at the door, my friend,
    A new face at the door.

ALFRED TENNYSON

93. LITTLE BILLEE

There were three sailors of Bristol city
Who took a boat and went to sea.
But first with beef and captain's biscuits
And pickled pork they loaded she.

There was gorging Jack and guzzling Jimmy,
And the youngest he was little Billee.
Now when they got so far as the Equator
They'd nothing left but one split pea.

Says gorging Jack to guzzling Jimmy,
"I am extremely hungaree."
To gorging Jack says guzzling Jimmy,
"We've nothing left, us must eat we."

Says gorging Jack to guzzling Jimmy,
"With one another, we shouldn't agree!
There's little Bill, he's young and tender,
We're old and tough, so let's eat he."

"Oh! Billy, we're going to kill and eat you,
So undo the button of your chemie."
When Bill received this information
He used his pocket-handkerchie.

"First let me say my catechism,
Which my poor mammy taught to me."
"Make haste, make haste," says guzzling Jimmy
While Jack pulled out his snickersnee.

So Billy went up to the main-topgallant mast,
And down he fell on his bended knee.
He scarce had come to the Twelfth Commandment
When up he jumps, "There's land I see.

"Jerusalem and Madagascar,
And North and South Amerikee:
There's the British flag a-riding at anchor,
With Admiral Napier, K.C.B."

So when they got aboard of the Admiral's
He hanged fat Jack and flogged Jimmee;
But as for little Bill, he made him
The Captain of a Seventy-three.

WILLIAM MAKEPEACE THACKERAY

94. LIFE, I KNOW NOT WHAT THOU ART

Life! I know not what thou art.
But know that thou and I must part;
And when, or how, or where we met,
I own to me's a secret yet.
Life! we've been long together
Through pleasant and through cloudy weather;
Tis hard to part when friends are dear--
Perhaps 'twill cost a sigh, a tear;
--Then steal away, give little warning,
Choose thine own time;
Say not Good Night,--but in some brighter clime
Bid me Good Morning.

ANNA L. BARBAULD

95. CROSSING THE BAR

Sunset and evening star,
And one clear call for me!
And may there be no moaning of the bar,
When I put out to sea,

But such a tide as moving seems asleep,
Too full for sound and foam,
When that which drew from out the boundless deep
Turns again home.

Twilight and evening bell,
And after that the dark!
And may there be no sadness of farewell,
When I embark;

For tho' from out our bourne of Time and Place
The flood may bear me far,
I hope to see my Pilot face to face
When I have cross'd the bar.

ALFRED TENNYSON

96. KRINKEN

Krinken was a little child,--
It was summer when he smiled.
Oft the hoary sea and grim
Stretched its white arms out to him,
Calling, "Sun-child, come to me;
Let me warm my heart with thee!"
But the child heard not the sea
Calling, yearning evermore
For the summer on the shore.

Krinken on the beach one day
Saw a maiden Nis at play;
On the pebbly beach she played
In the summer Krinken made.
Fair, and very fair, was she,
Just a little child was he.
"Krinken," said the maiden Nis,
"Let me have a little kiss,--
Just a kiss, and go with me
To the summer-lands that be
Down within the silver sea."

Krinken was a little child--
By the maiden Nis beguiled,
Hand in hand with her went he
And 'twas summer in the sea.
And the hoary sea and grim
To its bosom folded him--
Clasped and kissed the little form,
And the ocean's heart was warm.

Now the sea calls out no more;
It is winter on the shore,--
Winter where that little child
Made sweet summer when he smiled;
Though 'tis summer on the sea
Where with maiden Nis went he,--
It is winter on the shore,
Winter, winter evermore.
Of the summer on the deep
Come sweet visions in my sleep;
His fair face lifts from the sea,
His dear voice calls out to me,--
These my dreams of summer be.

Krinken was a little child,
By the maiden Nis beguiled;
Oft the hoary sea and grim
Reached its longing arms to him,
Crying, "Sim-child, come to me;
Let me warm my heart with thee!"
But the sea calls out no more;
It is winter on the shore,--
Winter, cold and dark and wild.
Krinken was a little child,--
It was summer when he smiled;
Down he went into the sea,
And the winter bides with me,
Just a little child was he.

EUGENE FIELD

97. THE CAPTAIN'S DAUGHTER

We were crowded in the cabin,
Not a soul would dare to sleep,--
It was midnight on the waters,
And a storm was on the deep.

'Tis a fearful thing in winter
To be shattered by the blast,
And to hear the rattling trumpet
Thunder, "Cut away the mast!"

So we shuddered there in silence,--
For the stoutest held his breath,
While the hungry sea was roaring
And the breakers talked with Death.

As thus we sat in darkness,
Each one busy with his prayers,
"We are lost!" the captain shouted
As he staggered down the stairs.

But his little daughter whispered,
As she took his icy hand,
"Isn't God upon the ocean,
Just the same as on the land?"

Then we kissed the little maiden.
And we spoke in better cheer,
And we anchored safe in harbour
When the morn was shining clear.

JAMES T. FIELDS

98. O CAPTAIN! MY CAPTAIN!

O Captain! my Captain! our fearful trip is done,
The ship has weathered every rack, the prize we sought is won,
The port is near, the bells I hear, the people all exulting,
While follow eyes the steady keel, the vessel grim and daring;
  But O heart! heart! heart!
   O the bleeding drops of red,
     Where on the deck my Captain lies,
       Fallen cold and dead.

O Captain! my Captain! rise up and hear the bells;
Rise up--for you the flag is flung--for you the bugle trills,
For you bouquets and ribboned wreaths-
                          -for you the shores a-crowding,
For you they call, the swaying mass, their eager faces turning;
  Here Captain! dear father!
   This arm beneath your head!
     It is some dream that on the deck
       You've fallen cold and dead.

My Captain does not answer, his lips are pale and still,
My father does not feel my arm, he has no pulse nor will.
The ship is anchored safe and sound, its voyage closed and done,
From fearful trip the victor ship comes in with object won;
  Exult O shores, and ring O bells!
   But I, with mournful tread,
     Walk the deck my Captain lies,
       Fallen cold and dead.

WALT WHITMAN

99. THE BURIAL OF SIR JOHN MOORE

Not a drum was heard, not a funeral note,
As his corse to the rampart we hurried;
Not a soldier discharged his farewell shot
O'er the grave where our hero we buried.

We buried him darkly at dead of night,
The sods with our bayonets turning;
By the struggling moonbeam's misty light,
And the lantern dimly burning.

No useless coffin enclosed his breast,
Not in sheet nor in shroud we wound him;
But he lay like a warrior taking his rest,
With his martial cloak around him.

Few and short were the prayers we said,
And we spoke not a word of sorrow;
But we steadfastly gazed on the face that was dead,
And we bitterly thought of the morrow.

We thought, as we hollowed his narrow bed,
And smoothed down his lonely pillow,
That the foe and the stranger would tread o'er his head,
And we far away on the billow!

Lightly they'll talk of the spirit that's gone,
And o'er his cold ashes upbraid him,--
But little he'll reck, if they let him sleep on
In the grave where a Briton has laid him.

But half of our heavy task was done
When the clock struck the hour for retiring;
And we heard the distant and random gun
That the foe was sullenly firing.

Slowly and sadly we laid him down,
From the field of his fame fresh and gory;
We carved not a line, and we raised not a stone--
But we left him alone with his glory!

CHARLES WOLFE

100. THE EPITAPH

Here rests his head upon the lap of Earth
A Youth to Fortune and to Fame unknown;
Fair Science frown'd not on his humble birth,
And Melancholy mark'd him for her own.

Large was his bounty, and his soul sincere,
Heaven did a recompense as largely send:
He gave to Mis'ry all he had, a tear:
He gain'd from Heav'n ('twas all he wish'd) a friend.

No farther seek his merits to disclose,
Or draw his frailties from their dread abode,
(There they alike in trembling hope repose,)
The bosom of his Father and his God.

THOMAS GRAY

INDEX OF POEMS

#

Thank you for reading my tribute to Classic Poetry. I hope you enjoyed it! It would mean the world to me if you could please take a moment to leave me a review at your favorite retailer.

If you wish to share any personal feedback directly with me, you can reach me at valeska@valeskamatti.com.

Remember you can also find this book in electronic format.

Thank you in advance! Stay safe.

Valeska Matti